TRUE IDENTITY

Scriptural Devotional

TRUE IDENTITY

Scriptural Devotional

CARRIE PICKETT

Published in partnership between Andrew Wommack Ministries and Harrison House Publishers

Shippensburg, PA 17257

ISBN 13 TP: 978-1-6675-0398-1

ISBN 13 eBook: 978-1-6675-0399-8

For Worldwide Distribution, Printed in the U.S.A.

1 2 3 4 5 6 7 8 / 27 26 25 24 23

To those who are willing to stand for the Lord, their faith, and to fight for the lost.

This is for you. May you stand firm in the identity you now possess as a child of God. In boldness may you not care about the opinions of the world but stand with joyful confidence of Christ in you.

Foreword

Your identity is the way you define yourself, or the way you let others define or characterize you as a person. It's the way you truly see yourself. Based on your perception of self, your lifestyle and attitude are developed and that becomes the way the world views you too.

Many times, identity can be a never-ending stage play—trying to portray an image of how we want others to see us. And unfortunately, the views of the audience are ever-changing, so your identity is ever-evolving, chasing the acceptance of others.

Will they like what they see today? Will the applause be enough for our soul and instill confidence? Will criticism cripple us to become slaves to ever-changing opinions?

The definitions of success are evasive. Once you think you've arrived on the floor of success you see that there are more floors of performance and expectations that lead to "fulfillment." This becomes an exhausting journey that many succumb to and never find the individual that they were created to be.

The goal of this scriptural devotional is that you would look in the mirror of the Word and see the glorious reflection of God's view of you! Your identity is not the way you grew up, your mistakes or successes along the way, your job, or your looks. Your identity is knowing you were created and fashioned by Almighty God. And not only do you possess eternal purposes and plans laid beforehand for you to live out, but you possess the greatest placement of identity imaginable: Christ Himself lives in you.

We are now called new creations in Christ Jesus. The old has passed away; behold, all has become new (1 Cor. 5:17). This blows away the world's boundaries that you are limited to—how you were raised or the career you possess.

The person of Christ, the fullness of the Godhead lives within you. Now your future is limitless because you have the power of the Kingdom of God with you.

This reality of salvation and right standing as a child of God terrifies the kingdom of darkness. The enemy looks at you and sees the temple of the Holy Spirit. Redeemed, righteous, sanctified, anointed, holy, filled with wisdom, understanding, power, and the gifts and fruits of God Himself.

Yet, the enemy also knows that many believers, despite this new covenant position and identity, don't truly know who they are. They struggle trying to "become" or "earn" their placement and blessings in Christ. The enemy is happy with that endeavor.

When we look into the mirror of the Word, we find the declarations of our identity proclaimed. Not as rules to obey, but gifts to be received. Will you choose today to believe what Jesus says about you? And will you lay down your emotions, failures, and views of yourself to believe you are more in Christ?

You and only you can say "amen" to the promises and declarations of who Christ has become in you. No one else can believe and stand for you. No one else can step into your God-given destiny. You own that privilege alone.

As you read the verses in this scriptural devotional, you will see God's view and redemption story spoken over you. Let your heart say *Amen! This is who I am! This is the real me!*

To you becoming who you were created to be—the world awaits...

Blessings and love,

Carrie Pickett

True Identity
SCRIPTURES

Psalm 62:6-7 ESV

He only is my rock and my salvation, my fortress; I shall not be shaken. On God rests my salvation and my glory; my mighty rock, my refuge is God.

Psalm 73:23-26 KJV

Nevertheless I am continually with thee: thou hast holden me by my right hand. Thou shalt guide me with thy counsel, and afterward receive me to glory. Whom have I in heaven but thee? and there is none upon earth that I desire beside thee. My flesh and my heart faileth: but God is the strength of my heart, and my portion for ever.

Psalm 103:1-5 KJV

Bless the Lord, O my soul: and all that is within me, bless his holy name. Bless the Lord, O my soul, and forget not all his benefits: Who forgiveth all thine iniquities; who healeth all thy diseases; Who redeemeth thy life from destruction; who crowneth thee with lovingkindness and tender mercies; Who satisfieth thy mouth with good things; so that thy youth is renewed like the eagle's.

Psalm 106:4-5 NKJV

*Remember me, O Lord, with the favor **You have toward** Your people. Oh, visit me with Your salvation, That I may see the benefit of Your chosen ones, That I may rejoice in the gladness of Your nation, That I may glory with Your inheritance.*

Psalm 115:14-15 KJV

The Lord shall increase you more and more, you and your children. Ye are blessed of the Lord which made heaven and earth.

Psalm 119:9-11 NKJV

How can a young man cleanse his way? By taking heed according to Your word. With my whole heart I have sought You; Oh, let me not wander from Your commandments! Your word I have hidden in my heart, That I might not sin against You.

Psalm 119:32 NKJV

I will run the course of Your commandments; For You shall enlarge my heart.

Psalm 119:44-45 NKJV

So shall I keep Your law continually, Forever and ever. And I will walk at liberty, For I seek Your precepts.

Psalm 119:46-47 NKJV

I will speak of Your testimonies also before kings, And will not be ashamed. And I will delight myself in Your commandments, Which I love.

Psalm 119:57-60 BSB

The LORD is my portion; I have promised to keep Your words. I have sought Your face with all my heart; be gracious to me according to Your promise. I considered my ways and turned my steps to Your testimonies. I hurried without hesitating to keep Your commandments.

1 Peter 3:15 BSB

But in your hearts sanctify Christ as Lord. Always be prepared to give a defense to everyone who asks you the reason for the hope that is in you. But respond with gentleness and respect,

1 Peter 4:10-11 NLT

God has given each of you a gift from his great variety of spiritual gifts. Use them well to serve one another. Do you have the gift of speaking? Then speak as though God himself were speaking through you. Do you have the gift of helping others? Do it with all the strength and energy that God supplies. Then everything you do will bring glory to God through Jesus Christ. All glory and power to him forever and ever! Amen.

1 Peter 5:5-7 KJV

Likewise, ye younger, submit yourselves unto the elder. Yea, all of you be subject one to another, and be clothed with humility: for God resisteth the proud, and giveth grace to the humble. Humble yourselves therefore under the mighty hand of God, that he may exalt you in due time: Casting all your care upon him; for he careth for you.

2 Peter 1:4 BSB

Through these He has given us His precious and magnificent promises, so that through them you may become partakers of the divine nature, now that you have escaped the corruption in the world caused by evil desires.

2 Peter 1:5-8 BSB

For this very reason, make every effort to add to your faith virtue; and to virtue, knowledge; and to knowledge, self-control; and to self-control, perseverance; and to perseverance, godliness; and to godliness, brotherly kindness; and to brotherly kindness, love. For if you possess these qualities and continue to grow in them, they will keep you from being ineffective and unproductive in your knowledge of our Lord Jesus Christ.

2 Peter 1:12-13 NKJV

For this reason I will not be negligent to remind you always of these things, though you know and are established in the present truth. Yes, I think it is right, as long as I am in this tent, to stir you up by reminding you,

2 Peter 3:11 AMP

Since all these things are to be destroyed in this way, what kind of people ought you to be [in the meantime] in holy behavior [that is, in a pattern of daily life that sets you apart as a believer] and in godliness [displaying profound reverence toward our awesome God],

1 John 4:15 KJV

Whosoever shall confess that Jesus is the Son of God, God dwelleth in him, and he in God.

1 John 5:12 KJV

He that hath the Son hath life; and he that hath not the Son of God hath not life.

1 John 5:13-14 KJV

These things have I written unto you that believe on the name of the Son of God; that ye may know that ye have eternal life, and that ye may believe on the name of the Son of God. And this is the confidence that we have in him, that, if we ask any thing according to his will, he heareth us:

1 Peter 1:18-19 BSB

For you know that it was not with perishable things such as silver or gold that you were redeemed from the empty way of life you inherited from your forefathers, but with the precious blood of Christ, a lamb without blemish or spot.

1 Peter 1:23 KJV

Being born again, not of corruptible seed, but of incorruptible, by the word of God, which liveth and abideth for ever.

1 Peter 2:9-10 NKJV

*But you **are** a chosen generation, a royal priesthood, a holy nation, His own special people, that you may proclaim the praises of Him who called you out of darkness into His marvelous light; who once **were** not a people but **are** now the people of God, who had not obtained mercy but now have obtained mercy.*

1 Peter 2:24 ESV

He himself bore our sins in his body on the tree, that we might die to sin and live to righteousness. By his wounds you have been healed.

2 Peter 1:3-4 ESV

His divine power has granted to us all things that pertain to life and godliness, through the knowledge of him who called us to his own glory and excellence, by which he has granted to us his precious and very great promises, so that through them you may become partakers of the divine nature, having escaped from the corruption that is in the world because of sinful desire.

1 John 2:12 AMP

I am writing to you, little children (believers, dear ones), because your sins have been forgiven for His name's sake [you have been pardoned and released from spiritual debt through His name because you have confessed His name, believing in Him as Savior].

1 John 2:20 AMP

But you have an anointing from the Holy One [you have been set apart, specially gifted and prepared by the Holy Spirit], and all of you know [the truth because He teaches us, illuminates our minds, and guards us from error].

1 John 2:27 ESV

But the anointing that you received from him abides in you, and you have no need that anyone should teach you. But as his anointing teaches you about everything, and is true, and is no lie—just as it has taught you, abide in him.

1 John 3:2 KJV

Beloved, now are we the sons of God, and it doth not yet appear what we shall be: but we know that, when he shall appear, we shall be like him; for we shall see him as he is.

1 John 3:22 NKJV

And whatever we ask we receive from Him, because we keep His commandments and do those things that are pleasing in His sight.

1 John 4:16-17 AMP

*We have come to know [by personal observation and experience], and have believed [with deep, consistent faith] the love which God has for us. God is love, and the one who abides in love abides in God, and God abides **continually** in him. In this [union and fellowship with Him], love is completed **and** perfected with us, so that we may have confidence in the day of judgment [with assurance and boldness to face Him]; because as He is, so are we in this world.*

1 John 5:20 AMP

*And we [have seen and] know [by personal experience] that the Son of God has [actually] come [to this world], and has given us understanding **and** insight so that we may [progressively and personally] know Him who is true; and we are in Him who is true—in His Son Jesus Christ. This is the true God and eternal life.*

Revelation 5:10 NKJV

And have made us kings and priests to our God; And we shall reign on the earth.

Revelation 12:11 KJV

And they overcame him by the blood of the Lamb, and by the word of their testimony; and they loved not their lives unto the death.

Ephesians 3:6 KJV

That the Gentiles should be fellowheirs, and of the same body, and partakers of his promise in Christ by the gospel:

Ephesians 4:7 AMP

Yet grace [God's undeserved favor] was given to each one of us [not indiscriminately, but in different ways] in proportion to the measure of Christ's [rich and abundant] gift.

Ephesians 4:24 AMP

and put on the new self [the regenerated and renewed nature], created in God's image, [godlike] in the righteousness and holiness of the truth [living in a way that expresses to God your gratitude for your salvation].

Philippians 4:13-15 AMP

*I can do all things [which He has called me to do]
through Him who strengthens **and** empowers me [to
fulfill His purpose—I am self-sufficient in Christ's
sufficiency; I am ready for anything and equal to
anything through Him who infuses me with inner
strength and confident peace.] Nevertheless, it was
right of you to share [with me] in my difficulties.
And you Philippians know that in the early days
of preaching the gospel, after I left Macedonia, no
church shared with me in the matter of giving and
receiving except you alone;*

Colossians 1:12-14 NKJV

*giving thanks to the Father who has qualified us
to be partakers of the inheritance of the saints in
the light. He has delivered us from the power of
darkness and conveyed **us** into the kingdom of
the Son of His love, in whom we have redemption
through His blood, the forgiveness of sins.*

Colossians 1:27 ESV

To them God chose to make known how great among the Gentiles are the riches of the glory of this mystery, which is Christ in you, the hope of glory.

Colossians 2:12-14 BSB

And having been buried with Him in baptism, you were raised with Him through your faith in the power of God, who raised Him from the dead. When you were dead in your trespasses and in the uncircumcision of your sinful nature, God made you alive with Christ. He forgave us all our trespasses, having canceled the debt ascribed to us in the decrees that stood against us. He took it away, nailing it to the cross!

Colossians 3:9-10 KJV

Lie not one to another, seeing that ye have put off the old man with his deeds; And have put on the new man, which is renewed in knowledge after the image of him that created him:

1 Thessalonians 5:4-6 KJV

But ye, brethren, are not in darkness, that that day should overtake you as a thief. Ye are all the children of light, and the children of the day: we are not of the night, nor of darkness. Therefore let us not sleep, as do others; but let us watch and be sober.

Hebrews 10:10 AMP

And in accordance with this will [of God] we [who believe in the message of salvation] have been sanctified [that is, set apart as holy for God and His purposes] through the offering of the body of Jesus Christ (the Messiah, the Anointed) once for all.

Hebrews 10:14 NIV

For by one sacrifice he has made perfect forever those who are being made holy.

Hebrews 13:5-6 BLB

Let your manner of life be without covetousness, being satisfied with the present; for He Himself has said: "Never will I leave you, never will I forsake you." So we are confident to say: "The Lord is my helper, and I will not be afraid; what shall man do to me?"

1 Peter 1:3-4 AMP

*Blessed [gratefully praised and adored] be the God and Father of our Lord Jesus Christ, who according to His abundant **and** boundless mercy has caused us to be born again [that is, to be reborn from above—spiritually transformed, renewed, and set apart for His purpose] to an ever-living hope **and** confident assurance through the resurrection of Jesus Christ from the dead, [born anew] into an inheritance which is imperishable [beyond the reach of change] and undefiled and unfading, reserved in heaven for you,*

1 Peter 1:16 KJV

Because it is written, Be ye holy; for I am holy.

1 Corinthians 3:9 BSB

For we are God's fellow workers; you are God's field, God's building.

1 Corinthians 3:16-17 KJV

Know ye not that ye are the temple of God, and that the Spirit of God dwelleth in you? If any man defile the temple of God, him shall God destroy; for the temple of God is holy, which temple ye are.

1 Corinthians 3:21-23 NKJV

*Therefore let no one boast in men. For all things are yours: whether Paul or Apollos or Cephas, or the world or life or death, or things present or things to come—all are yours. And you **are** Christ's, and Christ **is** God's.*

1 Corinthians 6:17 ESV

But he who is joined to the Lord becomes one spirit with him.

2 Corinthians 1:3-4 BSB

Blessed be the God and Father of our Lord Jesus Christ, the Father of compassion and the God of all comfort, who comforts us in all our troubles, so that we can comfort those in any trouble with the comfort we ourselves have received from God.

2 Corinthians 2:15 AMP

*For we are the **sweet** fragrance of Christ [which ascends] to God, [discernible both] among those who are being saved and among those who are perishing;*

2 Corinthians 3:3 NLT

Clearly, you are a letter from Christ showing the result of our ministry among you. This "letter" is written not with pen and ink, but with the Spirit of the living God. It is carved not on tablets of stone, but on human hearts.

2 Corinthians 3:6 BSB

And He has qualified us as ministers of a new covenant, not of the letter but of the Spirit; for the letter kills, but the Spirit gives life.

2 Corinthians 3:18 KJV

But we all, with open face beholding as in a glass the glory of the Lord, are changed into the same image from glory to glory, even as by the Spirit of the Lord.

2 Corinthians 5:6-7 AMP

So then, being always filled with good courage and confident hope, and knowing that while we are at home in the body we are absent from the Lord—for we walk by faith, not by sight [living our lives in a manner consistent with our confident belief in God's promises]—

2 Corinthians 5:17-21 AMP

*Therefore if anyone is in Christ [that is, grafted in, joined to Him by faith in Him as Savior], **he** is a new creature [reborn and renewed by the Holy Spirit]; the old things [the previous moral and spiritual condition] have passed away. Behold, new things have come [because spiritual awakening brings a new life]. But all **these** things are from God, who reconciled us to Himself through Christ [making us acceptable to Him] and gave us the ministry of reconciliation [so that by our example we might bring others to Him], that is, that God was in Christ reconciling the world to Himself, not counting people's sins against them [but canceling them]. And He has committed to us the message of reconciliation [that is, restoration to favor with God]. So we are ambassadors for Christ, as though God were making His appeal through us; we [as Christ's representatives] plead with you on behalf of Christ to be reconciled to God. He made Christ who knew no sin to [judicially] be sin on our behalf, so that in Him we would become the righteousness of God [that is, we would be made acceptable to Him and placed in a right relationship with Him by His gracious lovingkindness].*

2 Corinthians 9:8 NKJV

*And God **is** able to make all grace abound toward you, that you, always having all sufficiency in all **things**, may have an abundance for every good work.*

2 Corinthians 10:3-6 ESV

For though we walk in the flesh, we are not waging war according to the flesh. For the weapons of our warfare are not of the flesh but have divine power to destroy strongholds. We destroy arguments and every lofty opinion raised against the knowledge of God, and take every thought captive to obey Christ, being ready to punish every disobedience, when your obedience is complete.

Romans 6:2-6 ESV

By no means! How can we who died to sin still live in it? Do you not know that all of us who have been baptized into Christ Jesus were baptized into his death? We were buried therefore with him by baptism into death, in order that, just as Christ was raised from the dead by the glory of the Father, we too might walk in newness of life.

For if we have been united with him in a death like his, we shall certainly be united with him in a resurrection like his. We know that our old self was crucified with him in order that the body of sin might be brought to nothing, so that we would no longer be enslaved to sin.

Romans 6:11 NLT

So you also should consider yourselves to be dead to the power of sin and alive to God through Christ Jesus.

Romans 6:14 AMP

For sin will no longer be a master over you, since you are not under Law [as slaves], but under [unmerited] grace [as recipients of God's favor and mercy].

Romans 8:1-2 NIV

Therefore, there is now no condemnation for those who are in Christ Jesus, because through Christ Jesus the law of the Spirit who gives life has set you free from the law of sin and death.

Romans 8:16-17 ESV

The Spirit himself bears witness with our spirit that we are children of God, and if children, then heirs—heirs of God and fellow heirs with Christ, provided we suffer with him in order that we may also be glorified with him.

Romans 8:30-31 NKJV

*Moreover whom He predestined, these He also called; whom He called, these He also justified; and whom He justified, these He also glorified. What then shall we say to these things? If God is for us, who **can** be against us?*

Romans 8:38-39 ESV

For I am sure that neither death nor life, nor angels nor rulers, nor things present nor things to come, nor powers, nor height nor depth, nor anything else in all creation, will be able to separate us from the love of God in Christ Jesus our Lord.

Romans 14:8 NKJV

For if we live, we live to the Lord; and if we die, we die to the Lord. Therefore, whether we live or die, we are the Lord's.

Romans 15:14 ESV

I myself am satisfied about you, my brothers, that you yourselves are full of goodness, filled with all knowledge and able to instruct one another.

1 Corinthians 1:5-9 AMP

so that in everything you were [exceedingly] enriched in Him, in all speech [empowered by the spiritual gifts] and in all knowledge [with insight into the faith]. In this way our testimony about Christ was confirmed **and** *established in you, so that you are not lacking in any* **spiritual** *gift [which comes from the Holy Spirit], as you eagerly wait [with confident trust] for the revelation of our Lord Jesus Christ [when He returns]. And He will also confirm you to the end [keeping you strong and free of any accusation, so that you will be] blameless* **and** *beyond reproach in the day [of the return] of our Lord Jesus Christ. God is faithful [He is reliable, trustworthy and ever true to His promise—He can be depended on], and through Him you were called into fellowship with His Son, Jesus Christ our Lord.*

1 Corinthians 1:26-30 ESV

For consider your calling, brothers: not many of you were wise according to worldly standards, not many were powerful, not many were of noble birth. But God chose what is foolish in the world to shame the wise; God chose what is weak in the world to shame the strong; God chose what is low and despised in the world, even things that are not, to bring to nothing things that are, so that no human being might boast in the presence of God. And because of him you are in Christ Jesus, who became to us wisdom from God, righteousness and sanctification and redemption,

1 Corinthians 2:12 KJV

Now we have received, not the spirit of the world, but the spirit which is of God; that we might know the things that are freely given to us of God.

1 Corinthians 2:16 NLT

For, "Who can know the Lord's thoughts? Who knows enough to teach him?" But we understand these things, for we have the mind of Christ.

Psalm 8:4-8 NKJV

What is man that You are mindful of him, And the son of man that You visit him? For You have made him a little lower than the angels, And You have crowned him with glory and honor. You have made him to have dominion over the works of Your hands;

*You have put all **things** under his feet, All sheep and oxen—Even the beasts of the field, The birds of the air, And the fish of the sea That pass through the paths of the seas.*

Matthew 5:8 AMP

"Blessed [anticipating God's presence, spiritually mature] are the pure in heart [those with integrity, moral courage, and godly character], for they will see God.

Matthew 5:13-14 ESV

"You are the salt of the earth, but if salt has lost its taste, how shall its saltiness be restored? It is no longer good for anything except to be thrown out and trampled under people's feet. "You are the light of the world. A city set on a hill cannot be hidden.

John 5:24 BLB

Truly, truly, I say to you that the one hearing My word and believing the One having sent Me, he has eternal life and does not come into judgment, but has passed out of death into life.

John 7:38 AMP

*He who believes in Me [who adheres to, trusts in, and relies on Me], as the Scripture has said, 'From his innermost being will flow **continually** rivers of living water.'"*

John 8:31-32 KJV

Then said Jesus to those Jews which believed on him, If ye continue in my word, then are ye my disciples indeed; And ye shall know the truth, and the truth shall make you free.

John 14:20 NIV

On that day you will realize that I am in my Father, and you are in me, and I am in you.

John 16:15 BLB

All things that the Father has are Mine. Because of this, I said that He will take from that which is Mine and will disclose it to you.

John 16:27 NKJV

for the Father Himself loves you, because you have loved Me, and have believed that I came forth from God.

John 17:23 NKJV

I in them, and You in Me; that they may be made perfect in one, and that the world may know that You have sent Me, and have loved them as You have loved Me.

Romans 1:6-7 NLT

And you are included among those Gentiles who have been called to belong to Jesus Christ. I am writing to all of you in Rome who are loved by God and are called to be his own holy people. May God our Father and the Lord Jesus Christ give you grace and peace.

Romans 5:1-5 NLT

Therefore, since we have been made right in God's sight by faith, we have peace with God because of what Jesus Christ our Lord has done for us. Because of our faith, Christ has brought us into this place of undeserved privilege where we now stand, and we confidently and joyfully look forward to sharing God's glory. We can rejoice, too, when we run into problems and trials, for we know that they help us develop endurance. And endurance develops strength of character, and character strengthens our confident hope of salvation. And this hope will not lead to disappointment. For we know how dearly God loves us, because he has given us the Holy Spirit to fill our hearts with his love.

Romans 5:10 ESV

For if while we were enemies we were reconciled to God by the death of his Son, much more, now that we are reconciled, shall we be saved by his life.

Romans 5:17 NKJV

For if by the one man's offense death reigned through the one, much more those who receive abundance of grace and of the gift of righteousness will reign in life through the One, Jesus Christ.

Psalm 119:98-100 ESV

Your commandment makes me wiser than my enemies, for it is ever with me. I have more understanding than all my teachers, for your testimonies are my meditation. I understand more than the aged, for I keep your precepts.

Psalm 125:1 KJV

They that trust in the Lord shall be as mount Zion, which cannot be removed, but abideth for ever.

Psalm 139:13-16 BSB

For You formed my inmost being; You knit me together in my mother's womb. I praise You, for I am fearfully and wonderfully made. Marvelous are Your works, and I know this very well. My frame was not hidden from You when I was made in secret, when I was woven together in the depths of the earth. Your eyes saw my unformed body; all my days were written in Your book and ordained for me before one of them came to be.

Psalm 144:12-15 NKJV

*That our sons **may be** as plants grown up in their youth; That our daughters **may be** as pillars, Sculptured in palace style; **That** our barns **may be** full, Supplying all kinds of produce; **That** our sheep may bring forth thousands And ten thousands in our fields; **That** our oxen **may be** well laden; That there be no breaking in or going out; That there be no outcry in our streets. Happy **are** the people who are in such a state; Happy **are** the people whose God is the Lord!*

Psalm 146:3-6 KJV

Put not your trust in princes, nor in the son of man, in whom there is no help. His breath goeth forth, he returneth to his earth; in that very day his thoughts perish. Happy is he that hath the God of Jacob for his help, whose hope is in the Lord his God: Which made heaven, and earth, the sea, and all that therein is: which keepeth truth for ever:

Psalm 147:13-15 ESV

For he strengthens the bars of your gates; he blesses your children within you. He makes peace in your borders; he fills you with the finest of the wheat. He sends out his command to the earth; his word runs swiftly.

Romans 9:25-26 NLT

Concerning the Gentiles, God says in the prophecy of Hosea, "Those who were not my people, I will now call my people. And I will love those whom I did not love before."

And, "Then, at the place where they were told, 'You are not my people,' there they will be called 'children of the living God.'"

Romans 10:11 AMP

For the Scripture says, "Whoever believes in Him [whoever adheres to, trusts in, and relies on Him] will not be disappointed [in his expectations]."

Romans 12:1-2 NIV

Therefore, I urge you, brothers and sisters, in view of God's mercy, to offer your bodies as a living sacrifice, holy and pleasing to God—this is your true and proper worship. Do not conform to the pattern of this world, but be transformed by the renewing of your mind. Then you will be able to test and approve what God's will is—his good, pleasing and perfect will.

Romans 12:4-6 BSB

Just as each of us has one body with many members, and not all members have the same function, so in Christ we who are many are one body, and each member belongs to one another. We have different gifts according to the grace given us. If one's gift is prophecy, let him use it in proportion to his faith;

1 Corinthians 1:4-5 ESV

I give thanks to my God always for you because of the grace of God that was given you in Christ Jesus, that in every way you were enriched in him in all speech and all knowledge—

1 Corinthians 2:4 KJV

And my speech and my preaching was not with enticing words of man's wisdom, but in demonstration of the Spirit and of power:

1 Corinthians 6:19-20 NKJV

*Or do you not know that your body is the temple of the Holy Spirit **who** is in you, whom you have from God, and you are not your own? For you were bought at a price; therefore glorify God in your body and in your spirit, which are God's.*

1 Corinthians 12:18 KJV

But now hath God set the members every one of them in the body, as it hath pleased him.

1 Corinthians 12:27 NKJV

Now you are the body of Christ, and members individually.

2 Corinthians 3:12 AMP

Since we have such a [glorious] hope and confident expectation, we speak with great courage,

2 Corinthians 4:7-12 AMP

*But we have this **precious** treasure [the good news about salvation] in [unworthy] earthen vessels [of human frailty], so that the grandeur **and** surpassing greatness of the power will be [shown to be] from God [His sufficiency] and not from ourselves. We are pressured in every way [hedged in], but not crushed; perplexed [unsure of finding a way out], but not driven to despair; hunted down **and** persecuted, but not deserted [to stand alone]; struck down, but never destroyed; always carrying around in the body the dying of Jesus, so that the [resurrection] life of Jesus also may be shown in our body. For we who live are constantly [experiencing the threat of] being handed over to death for Jesus' sake, so that the [resurrection] life of Jesus also may be evidenced in our mortal body [which is subject to death]. So **physical** death is [actively] at work in us, but [spiritual] life [is actively at work] in you.*

Galatians 2:19-20 NLT

For when I tried to keep the law, it condemned me. So I died to the law—I stopped trying to meet all its requirements—so that I might live for God. My old self has been crucified with Christ. It is no longer I who live, but Christ lives in me. So I live in this earthly body by trusting in the Son of God, who loved me and gave himself for me.

Galatians 3:26 AMP

For you [who are born-again have been reborn from above—spiritually transformed, renewed, sanctified and] are all children of God [set apart for His purpose with full rights and privileges] through faith in Christ Jesus.

Galatians 3:29 KJV

And if ye be Christ's, then are ye Abraham's seed, and heirs according to the promise.

Galatians 4:6-7 BSB

And because you are sons, God sent the Spirit of His Son into our hearts, crying out, "Abba, Father!" So you are no longer a slave, but a son; and since you are a son, you are also an heir through God.

Galatians 5:22-24 KJV

But the fruit of the Spirit is love, joy, peace, longsuffering, gentleness, goodness, faith, Meekness, temperance: against such there is no law. And they that are Christ's have crucified the flesh with the affections and lusts.

Ephesians 1:2-7 AMP

*Grace to you and peace [inner calm and spiritual well-being] from God our Father and the Lord Jesus Christ. Blessed **and** worthy of praise be the God and Father of our Lord Jesus Christ, who has blessed us with every spiritual blessing in the heavenly realms in Christ, just as [in His love] He chose us in Christ [actually selected us for Himself as His own] before the foundation of the world, so that we would be holy [that is, consecrated, set apart for Him, purpose-driven] and blameless in His sight. In love He predestined **and** lovingly planned for us to be adopted to Himself as [His own] children through Jesus Christ, in accordance with the kind intention **and** good pleasure of His will—to the praise of His glorious grace **and** favor, which He so freely bestowed on us in the Beloved [His Son, Jesus Christ]. In Him we have redemption [that is, our deliverance and salvation] through His blood, [which paid the penalty for our sin and resulted in] the forgiveness **and** complete pardon of our sin, in accordance with the riches of His grace*

Ephesians 1:11 AMP

*In Him also we have received an inheritance [a destiny—we were claimed by God as His own], having been predestined (chosen, appointed beforehand) according to the purpose of Him who works everything in agreement with the counsel **and** design of His will,*

Ephesians 1:13-14 NKJV

*In Him you also **trusted**, after you heard the word of truth, the gospel of your salvation; in whom also, having believed, you were sealed with the Holy Spirit of promise, who is the guarantee of our inheritance until the redemption of the purchased possession, to the praise of His glory.*

Ephesians 2:4-10 AMP

*But God, being [so very] rich in mercy, because of His great **and** wonderful love with which He loved us, even when we were [spiritually] dead **and** separated from Him because of our sins, He made us [spiritually] alive together with Christ (for by His grace—His undeserved favor and mercy— you have been saved from God's judgment). And He raised us up together with Him [when we believed], and seated us with Him in the heavenly **places**, [because we are] in Christ Jesus, [and He did this] so that in the ages to come He might [clearly] show the immeasurable and unsurpassed riches of His grace in [His] kindness toward us in Christ Jesus [by providing for our redemption]. For it is by grace [God's remarkable compassion and favor drawing you to Christ] that you have been saved [actually delivered from judgment and given eternal life] through faith. And this [salvation] is not of yourselves [not through your own effort], but it is the [undeserved, gracious] gift of God; not as a result of [your] works [nor your attempts to keep the Law], so that no one will [be able to] boast or take credit in any way [for his salvation]. For we*

are His workmanship [His own master work, a work of art], created in Christ Jesus [reborn from above—spiritually transformed, renewed, ready to be used] for good works, which God prepared [for us] beforehand [taking paths which He set], so that we would walk in them [living the good life which He prearranged and made ready for us].

Ephesians 2:13-14 ESV

But now in Christ Jesus you who once were far off have been brought near by the blood of Christ. For he himself is our peace, who has made us both one and has broken down in his flesh the dividing wall of hostility

Ephesians 2:19-22 AMP

So then you are no longer strangers and aliens [outsiders without rights of citizenship], but you are fellow citizens with the saints (God's people), and are [members] of God's household, having been built on the foundation of the apostles and prophets, with Christ Jesus Himself as the [chief] Cornerstone, in whom the whole structure is joined together, and it continues [to increase] growing into a holy temple in the Lord [a sanctuary dedicated, set apart, and sacred to the presence of the Lord]. In Him [and in fellowship with one another] you also are being built together into a dwelling place of God in the Spirit.

2 Corinthians 5:14-15 ESV

For the love of Christ controls us, because we have concluded this: that one has died for all, therefore all have died; and he died for all, that those who live might no longer live for themselves but for him who for their sake died and was raised.

2 Corinthians 6:14-16 ESV

Do not be unequally yoked with unbelievers. For what partnership has righteousness with lawlessness? Or what fellowship has light with darkness? What accord has Christ with Belial? Or what portion does a believer share with an unbeliever? What agreement has the temple of God with idols? For we are the temple of the living God; as God said, "I will make my dwelling among them and walk among them, and I will be their God, and they shall be my people.

Psalm 1:1-3 NKJV

*Blessed **is** the man Who walks not in the counsel of the ungodly, Nor stands in the path of sinners, Nor sits in the seat of the scornful; But his delight **is** in the law of the Lord, And in His law he meditates day and night. He shall be like a tree Planted by the rivers of water, That brings forth its fruit in its season, Whose leaf also shall not wither; And whatever he does shall prosper.*

Psalm 2:7-8 BSB

I will proclaim the decree spoken to Me by the LORD: "You are My Son; today I have become Your Father. Ask Me, and I will make the nations Your inheritance, the ends of the earth Your possession.

Psalm 5:11-12 ESV

But let all who take refuge in you rejoice; let them ever sing for joy, and spread your protection over them, that those who love your name may exult in you. For you bless the righteous, O Lord; you cover him with favor as with a shield.

Psalm 26:12 NLT

Now I stand on solid ground, and I will publicly praise the Lord.

Psalm 28:7 KJV

The Lord is my strength and my shield; my heart trusted in him, and I am helped: therefore my heart greatly rejoiceth; and with my song will I praise him.

Psalm 101:2-4 NKJV

I will behave wisely in a perfect way. Oh, when will You come to me? I will walk within my house with a perfect heart. I will set nothing wicked before my eyes;

I hate the work of those who fall away; It shall not cling to me. A perverse heart shall depart from me; I will not know wickedness.

Acts 2:38-39 BSB

Peter replied, "Repent and be baptized, every one of you, in the name of Jesus Christ for the forgiveness of your sins, and you will receive the gift of the Holy Spirit. This promise belongs to you and your children and to all who are far off—to all whom the Lord our God will call to Himself."

Acts 17:28 NKJV

for in Him we live and move and have our being, as also some of your own poets have said, 'For we are also His offspring.'

Galatians 1:10 ESV

For am I now seeking the approval of man, or of God? Or am I trying to please man? If I were still trying to please man, I would not be a servant of Christ.

Galatians 1:15 ESV

But when he who had set me apart before I was born, and who called me by his grace,

Galatians 4:9 NKJV

But now after you have known God, or rather are known by God, how is it that you turn again to the weak and beggarly elements, to which you desire again to be in bondage?

Ephesians 1:17-18 AMP

*[I always pray] that the God of our Lord Jesus Christ, the Father of glory, may grant you a spirit of wisdom and of revelation [that gives you a deep and personal and intimate insight] into the true knowledge of Him [for we know the Father through the Son]. And [I pray] that the eyes of your heart [the very center and core of your being] may be enlightened [flooded with light by the Holy Spirit], so that you will know **and** cherish the hope [the divine guarantee, the confident expectation] to which He has called you, the riches of His glorious inheritance in the saints (God's people),*

Ephesians 3:7-8 ESV

Of this gospel I was made a minister according to the gift of God's grace, which was given me by the working of his power. To me, though I am the very least of all the saints, this grace was given, to preach to the Gentiles the unsearchable riches of Christ,

Ephesians 3:12 BSB

In Him and through faith in Him we may enter God's presence with boldness and confidence.

Ephesians 4:1-2 AMP

So I, the prisoner for the Lord, appeal to you to live a life worthy of the calling to which you have been called [that is, to live a life that exhibits godly character, moral courage, personal integrity, and mature behavior—a life that expresses gratitude to God for your salvation], with all humility [forsaking self-righteousness], and gentleness [maintaining self-control], with patience, bearing with one another in [unselfish] love.

Ephesians 4:22-24 AMP

*that, regarding your previous way of life, you put off your old self [completely discard your former nature], which is being corrupted through deceitful desires, and be **continually** renewed in the spirit of your mind [having a fresh, untarnished mental and spiritual attitude], and put on the new self [the regenerated and renewed nature], created in God's image, [godlike] in the righteousness and holiness of the truth [living in a way that expresses to God your gratitude for your salvation].*

Ephesians 5:25-27 ESV

Husbands, love your wives, as Christ loved the church and gave himself up for her, that he might sanctify her, having cleansed her by the washing of water with the word, so that he might present the church to himself in splendor, without spot or wrinkle or any such thing, that she might be holy and without blemish.

Ephesians 6:5-7 ESV

Bondservants, obey your earthly masters with fear and trembling, with a sincere heart, as you would Christ, not by the way of eye-service, as people-pleasers, but as bondservants of Christ, doing the will of God from the heart, rendering service with a good will as to the Lord and not to man,

Ephesians 6:10-18 NKJV

*Finally, my brethren, be strong in the Lord and in the power of His might. Put on the whole armor of God, that you may be able to stand against the wiles of the devil. For we do not wrestle against flesh and blood, but against principalities, against powers, against the rulers of the darkness of this age, against spiritual **hosts** of wickedness in the heavenly **places**. Therefore take up the whole armor of God, that you may be able to withstand in the evil day, and having done all, to stand. Stand therefore, having girded your waist with truth, having put on the breastplate of righteousness, and having shod your feet with the preparation of the gospel of peace; above all, taking the shield of faith with which you will be able to quench all the fiery darts of the wicked one. And take the helmet of salvation, and the sword of the Spirit, which is the word of God; praying always with all prayer and supplication in the Spirit, being watchful to this end with all perseverance and supplication for all the saints—*

1 John 5:20 NKJV

And we know that the Son of God has come and has given us an understanding, that we may know Him who is true; and we are in Him who is true, in His Son Jesus Christ. This is the true God and eternal life.

Colossians 2:2 BSB

that they may be encouraged in heart, knit together in love, and filled with the full riches of complete understanding, so that they may know the mystery of God, namely Christ,

Colossians 3:15-17 ESV

And let the peace of Christ rule in your hearts, to which indeed you were called in one body. And be thankful. Let the word of Christ dwell in you richly, teaching and admonishing one another in all wisdom, singing psalms and hymns and spiritual songs, with thankfulness in your hearts to God. And whatever you do, in word or deed, do everything in the name of the Lord Jesus, giving thanks to God the Father through him.

1 Thessalonians 2:4 ESV

but just as we have been approved by God to be entrusted with the gospel, so we speak, not to please man, but to please God who tests our hearts.

1 Timothy 6:11-12 AMP

But as for you, O man of God, flee from these things; aim at and pursue righteousness [true goodness, moral conformity to the character of God], godliness [the fear of God], faith, love, steadfastness, and gentleness. Fight the good fight of the faith [in the conflict with evil]; take hold of the eternal life to which you were called, and [for which] you made the good confession [of faith] in the presence of many witnesses.

2 Timothy 1:9 BSB

He has saved us and called us to a holy calling, not because of our works, but by His own purpose and by the grace He granted us in Christ Jesus before time began.

2 Timothy 1:12 ESV

which is why I suffer as I do. But I am not ashamed, for I know whom I have believed, and I am convinced that he is able to guard until that day what has been entrusted to me.

Hebrews 10:39 NKJV

But we are not of those who draw back to perdition, but of those who believe to the saving of the soul.

Hebrews 11:6 ESV

And without faith it is impossible to please him, for whoever would draw near to God must believe that he exists and that he rewards those who seek him.

Hebrews 12:1 NKJV

Therefore we also, since we are surrounded by so great a cloud of witnesses, let us lay aside every weight, and the sin which so easily ensnares us, and let us run with endurance the race that is set before us,

1 Peter 2:4-5 NKJV

*Coming to Him as to a living stone, rejected indeed by men, but chosen by God **and** precious, you also, as living stones, are being built up a spiritual house, a holy priesthood, to offer up spiritual sacrifices acceptable to God through Jesus Christ.*

Zephaniah 3:17 NIV

The Lord your God is with you, the Mighty Warrior who saves. He will take great delight in you; in his love he will no longer rebuke you, but will rejoice over you with singing."

Isaiah 44:3 ESV

For I will pour water on the thirsty land, and streams on the dry ground; I will pour my Spirit upon your offspring, and my blessing on your descendants.

Isaiah 58:11 NIV

The Lord will guide you always; he will satisfy your needs in a sun-scorched land and will strengthen your frame. You will be like a well-watered garden, like a spring whose waters never fail.

Receive Jesus as Your Savior

Choosing to receive Jesus Christ as your Lord and Savior is the most important decision you'll ever make!

God's Word promises, *"That if thou shalt confess with thy mouth the Lord Jesus, and shalt believe in thine heart that God hath raised him from the dead, thou shalt be saved. For with the heart man believeth unto righteousness; and with the mouth confession is made unto salvation"* (Rom. 10:9–10). *"For whosoever shall call upon the name of the Lord shall be saved"* (Rom. 10:13). By His grace, God has already done everything to provide salvation. Your part is simply to believe and receive.

Pray out loud: "Jesus, I confess that You are my Lord and Savior. I believe in my heart that God raised You from the dead. By faith in Your Word, I receive salvation now. Thank You for saving me."

The very moment you commit your life to Jesus Christ, the truth of His Word instantly comes to pass in your spirit. Now that you're born again, there's a brand-new you!

Receive the
Holy Spirit

As His child, your loving heavenly Father wants to give you the supernatural power you need to live a new life. *"For every one that asketh receiveth; and he that seeketh findeth; and to him that knocketh it shall be opened…how much more shall your heavenly Father give the Holy Spirit to them that ask him?"* (Luke 11:10–13).

All you have to do is ask, believe, and receive!

Pray this: "Father, I recognize my need for Your power to live a new life. Please fill me with Your Holy Spirit. By faith, I receive it right now. Thank You for baptizing me. Holy Spirit, You are welcome in my life."

Congratulations! Now you're filled with God's supernatural power.

Some syllables from a language you don't recognize will rise up from your heart to your mouth (1 Cor. 14:14). As you speak them out loud by faith, you're releasing God's power from within and building yourself up in the spirit (1 Cor. 14:4). You can do this whenever and wherever you like.

It doesn't really matter whether you felt anything or not when you prayed to receive the Lord and His Spirit. If you believed in your heart that you received, then God's Word promises you did. *"Therefore I say unto you, What things soever ye desire, when ye pray, believe that ye receive them, and ye shall have them"* (Mark 11:24). God always honors His Word—believe it!

Please contact me and let me know that you've prayed to receive Jesus as your Savior or be filled with the Holy Spirit. I would like to rejoice with you and help you understand more fully what has taken place in your life. I'll send you a free gift that will help you understand and grow in your new relationship with the Lord.

Welcome to your new life!

Call for Prayer

If you need prayer for any reason, you can call our Prayer Line 24 hours a day, seven days a week at 719-635-1111. A trained prayer minister will answer your call and pray with you. Every day, we receive testimonies of healings and other miracles from our Prayer Line, and we are ministering God's nearly-too-good-to-be-true message of the Gospel to more people than ever. So I encourage you to call today!

God has more for you.

e you longing to find your God-given purpose? At Charis Bible College
you will establish a firm foundation in the Word of God and receive
hands-on ministry experience to **find, follow** and **fulfill** your purpose.

**Scan the QR code to visit
CharisBibleCollege.org**

Admissions@awmcharis.com
(844) 360-9577

Change your life. **Change the world.**

life FOUNDATIONS
with Carrie Pickett

Join Carrie as she uncovers the foundational principles of the Word of God and discover how these truths can transform your everyday life.

Scan the QR code to watch full episodes of Life Foundations

CONTACT INFORMATION

Charis Bible College

800 Gospel Truth Way

Woodland Park, CO 80863

info@charisbiblecollege.org

Helpline Available 24/7: 719-635-1111

CharisBibleCollege.org

Also visit Carrie at: CarriePickett.com